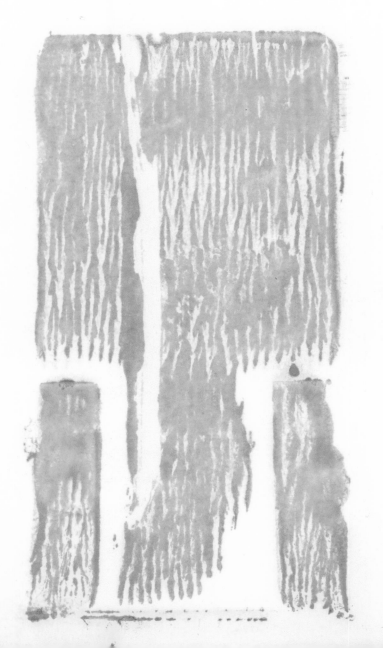

THE WARSAW GHETTO

THE WARSAW GHETTO

Drawings by Józef Kaliszan

Compiled and Edited by Czeslaw Z. Banasiewicz

Thomas Yoseloff

New York • South Brunswick • London

Thomas Yoseloff, Publisher
Cranbury, New Jersey 08512

Thomas Yoseloff Ltd
18 Charing Cross Road
London W.C. 2, England

6782
Printed in the United States of America

THE WARSAW GHETTO

Józef Kaliszan

BIOGRAPHICAL NOTE

Jozef Kaliszan was born on January 6, 1927 in Wilchin, in the Poznan region of Poland. He spent his childhood here and neither he nor those close to him attached great importance to his passion for drawing.

On September 1, 1939 he did not pass his high school entrance examination in time to become a student: war had broken out with Germany. His father became a prisoner of war in the first months of the war. The Germans occupied Poznan, which then became a German town, under the name of Posen. The Kaliszan family was evicted from their home which was now in the German sector; the high school gates were closed to Polish children. Instead, forced labor was proclaimed for women and children over fourteen. In 1940 Kaliszan began his apprenticeship with a German blacksmith. After a year, in spite of his strong physique, ten hours of daily physical labor at the anvil impaired his health. His mother did everything to find a different job for him. The only relaxation he had was the time he spent on Sundays in the little streets of the old city and on the banks of the Warta with his sketch pad.

In 1942 Kaliszan became assistant to the locksmith at the Poznan Opera. His health improved and he was able to continue his studies at classes held in secret. The opportunity to earn a little extra allowed him to buy paints. He painted, learned to sing, and also formed a conspiracy with his colleagues. They organized help for the prisoners near Poznan.

In February, 1945, the battles for Poznan began. During the bombardments and artillery shellings many people perished and houses became rubble. After two weeks of living as a nomad in a cellar Kaliszan came out of the ruins of his temporary home to make his way with his mother, younger brother, and a grandmother into a safer sector.

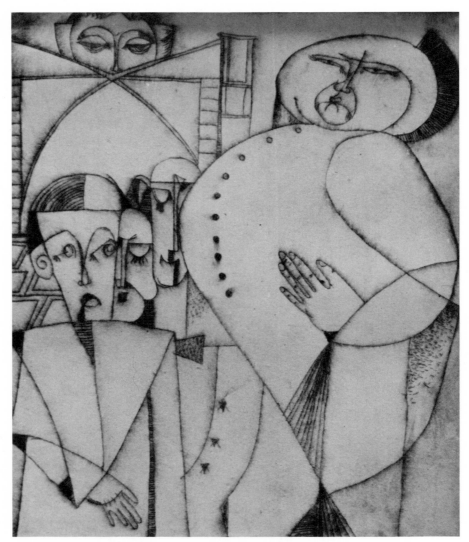

ACTOR ON A COUNTRY TOUR. ENGRAVING, 1956.

In May of the same year Kaliszan enrolled in the Higher School of Plastic
Arts.

Kaliszan graduated from the State Higher School of Plastic Arts in 1950.
After pre-degree practice under Prof. Xawery Dunikowski he worked on his
degree with Prof. Bazyl Wojtowicz, and then became his assistant at the
school. At a country-wide contest for the Chopin monument he achieved
recognition.

In 1951 he won second prize in the contest for a new monument of Chopin
in Warsaw. (The first prize was not given. At the suggestion of the committee
it was decided to reconstruct the Lazienki monument destroyed by the
Nazis.)

From 1950 on he took part in semi-annual exhibits of the Society of Polish Plastic Artists of the Poznan region.

In 1952 Kaliszan executed three bas-reliefs and carved a medallion in the Old Market in Poznan; he also took part in a country-wide exhibition by young people.

The first exhibition by an individual of graphic arts and drawing took place in the hall of the International Press and Book Club in Poznan, in 1954.

In 1955 he achieved recognition at a contest for his "Monument to Liberation" in Wroclaw.

STILL-LIFE. WOODCUT, 1956.

In 1956 he broke ties with P.W.S.S.P. (State Higher School of Plastic Arts) in Poznan, because his studies at school took up too much of his time. He felt that the everyday routine of learning formal theory and composition together with the other students was a waste of his time. As one of the co-founders of the Poznan group of R-55 he took part in their first exhibition, whose theme was "Still Life." The purpose of the group was stated in the introduction to

9

HELIOS (THE SUN). COPPER SCULPTURE, 1964. (COURTESY OF KUCHARSKI)

the catalog: "The aim of the exhibition is to find a level of recognition on which the objects observed would be in different perspectives at the moment of active co-existence of the still life and the live object; to find the moment of transfer of the idea of one object and its function into the atmosphere of the other object."

10

In a survey in *Cultural Review* of May 10, 1966, Wieslaw Rustecki wrote among other things:
"The works of Józef Kaliszan evoke great interest. An artist whose works we remember from numerous Warsaw exhibitions is exhibiting, besides his graphic works, two attempts at carving. I say "attempts" because it is difficult

TRANSLUCENT SCULPTURE. PLEXIGLASS, 1964.

11

to speak here of pure sculpture. Both "The Explosion of Redness" and "The Dying Flower" (polychromic plaster) are interesting studies bordering on both painting and sculpture. The plastic "still life," solving problems of painting, color shading, while maintaining a clarity of drawing, rather supports our supposition. Kaliszan's plasters are experiments in the world of "mixed techniques" and are all the more fortunate because they are really successful."

BAS RELIEF WITH EPITAPH BY ROZEWICZ. COPPER & GLASS, 1964.
(COURTESY OF KUCHARSKI)

At the time this exhibition was taking place, Józef Kaliszan's sculpture was being exhibited at the Old City Hall of Culture in Warsaw. Kira Galczynska wrote in the Polish Courier on May 8, 1956: "His creative medium is neither stone, plaster or even clay. His work I would call 'compositions in wood' (although no text by the author accompanies them). They are color planes connected to one another, forming curious shapes, and the intentional deformation produces interesting effects. The hues of the wood, distinct and clear and free of any similarity, are based on a mere allusion to the subject; they do not suggest anything, yet at the same time give a pleasant visual sen-

CONSTRUCT PAINTINGS 1 & 2. FROM WARSAW EXHIBITION, 1959.

13

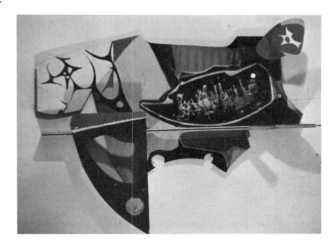

sation. The aim of the artist was to use the grain of the wood, showing the effects which raw untreated wood could create."

In 1957 a television studio opened in Poznan. Kaliszan began his connection with T.V. as a set designer. At the same time he received a grant to go to Egypt. He exhibited his graphic works in Cairo and Alexandria, and on the return trip had an opportunity to test his knowledge of the history of art during a visit to Italy.

EXPRESSION IN OUR CITY, FROM SERIES, GROWTH, ENGRAVING, 1956.

COMPOSITION. MONOTYPIA, 1959.

After his return his compiled sketches and impressions formed two distinct cycles. An exhibition of gouache was held in Poznan.

In 1958 his monotypes were exhibited in Poznan, then were partially transferred to Sofia (Bulgaria) at a later date.

In 1959 there was an exhibition of his monotypes and watercolors in Hamburg in the exhibition hall of the Congress of Freedom of Culture. The Hamburg *Abendblatt* of October 7, 1959, said: "The Hamburg exhibit shows him as a painter, a graphic artist and a set designer. His trip to Cairo not only exerted influence on the sweep and expression of the contour of his pictures ("Odalisque from the Palace of the Calif") but also influenced his later paintings 'Bazaar' and 'Towns' which as far as their composition is concerned remain under the influence of the Arab world, revealing it to us in all its traditions. Kaliszan loves bright, shining and penetrating watercolors

15

COMPOSITION. MONOTYPIA, 1959.

which he seldom mellows down with white." When painting subjects he explains form (or shape) through strong, rythmic movement. In subject monotypes color is all important, and acting through a delicate distribution of shades, mainly green and greyish-white, achieved individual expression. The clear and 'ringing' combination of colors is achieved as a result of conscious, planned, creative discipline. These works are from the period 1956-1959.
From *Die Welt* of September 16, 1959: Kaliszan reveals various possibilities for artistic creation at an unusually fast pace. His water colors, which sometimes hint at Paul Klee, are compositions of planes with fragments of subjects. Sometimes in the composition and color there is a feeling of dilettantism, probably caused by his search in a new and unfamiliar territory. His humor is revealed in the Picasso-like dancers 'The Odalisques' who came into being in Egypt. The most attractive are the new abstract monotypes in which the artist freely composes in color."

16

COMPOSITION. MONOTYPIA, 1959.

In 1960 Kaliszan, the set designer, signed a contract with the A. Fredro Theater in Gniezno, while at the same time he was designing settings for television productions. To his better achievements of this period belong the set designs for the plays *The Blacksmith and the Stars* by Szaniawski (for T.V.), *The Alchemist* by Ben Jonson (for the theater), the previews of Shakespeare's *Pericles, Prince of Tyre* (theater), *Marius* by Pagniot (T.V.). The friendly halls of the M. P. & K. club in Poznan, of which Kaliszan had grown particularly fond, hosted two separate exhibitions of compositions in fabrics.

In 1961 he painted a cycle of color monotypes entitled "The history of one little window pane."

COMPOSITION. MONOTYPIA, 1959.

In 1962 an individual exhibition of sculpture took place in the Poznan hall of Z.P.A.P. with the utilitarian title "Concrete and glass." Jacek Juszczyk, a plastic arts critic of the Poznan Gazette wrote: "Józef Kaliszan, with a great deal of ingenuity, uses materials still little known in sculpture, such as glass, or, slightly better known, concrete and sheet metal. His creations from glass blocks are beautiful, with opalescent hues of green, in places almost black. This is not a single piece of glass pane but rather a rough glass with an irregular surface, hardly even crystallized at many points, that he uses. Combined with either metal or concrete, his creations form a harmonized whole in spite of visible differences in materials. The use of these materials (iron,

LIBERATION. BRONZE SCULPTURE, 1963.

concrete and glass) elevates them from mere common substances. They now
exist in a different setting, in a realm already governed by the rules of art.
Kaliszan creates from a simple material such as iron (simple in the general
sense of its use) fantastic birds or huge insects, or even deities with anthropo-

19

morphic characteristics. These creations are light, yet full of dignity ("Symbolic form") expressing in a poetic manner the possibilities of the material from which they were formed. The search continues for a means of blending harmoniously the various materials. As an example there is a large lens of plastic and water (1) smooth and opalescent amid raw rough frames of

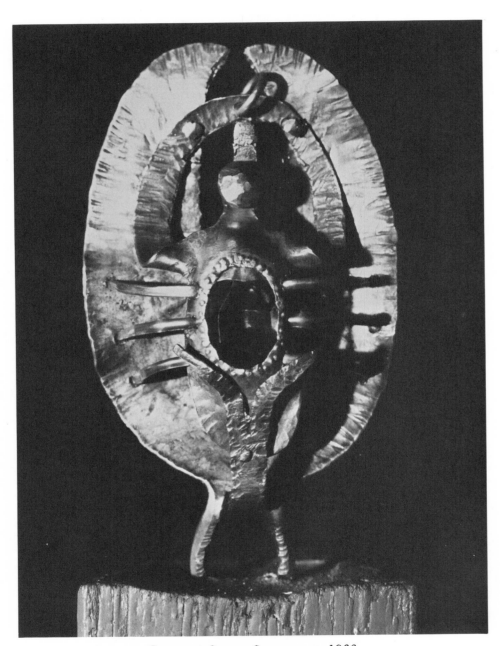

OBERON. SILVER SCULPTURE, 1966.

THE CAT AND THE LANTERNS. COPPERPLATE, 1955.

concrete. These works, from their conception through their execution, are close to life, and the connection is deeper than a superficial critic might think."

Following the success of the exhibition Kaliszan executed a bas relief in glass and concrete for one of the Poznan schools ("Astrolabium" 1962). He also exhibited colored graphics in Koszalin.

In 1963 a new exhibition hall in Poznan in the Palace of Culture was opened with drawings from Jugoslavia and monotypes by J. Kaliszan.

In 1964 an exhibition of artistic medals and jewellery was held in Arezzo (Italy).

An exhibition took place in the M. P. & K. Club of "Small Sculpture Forms" (river stones or pebbles). Jacek Juszczyk wrote in the Poznan *Gazette* of December 11, 1964: "Józef Kaliszan is exhibiting carvings small in size yet each easily capable of fulfilling the role of a miniature work of art, which anybody visiting the exhibition would be pleased to have in their home. Various inspirations lie behind these creations. They run the entire gamut of

GARLIC AND BASKET. DRY-POINT, 1956.

THE GOLDEN HEAD. GILDED PLASTER, 1955.

THE POLYCHROMED HEAD. MAJOLIKA, 1956.

styles. From the first carving reminiscent of the so-called 'Venus of Willendorf' through the archaic Greek and Egyptian sculpture, tiny sacral figures of India, Chinese figurines, Negro masks, up to contemporary non-figurative exercises.

This artist from Poznan is a very contrary creator. This time his differences are kept within the confines of uniform ideas."

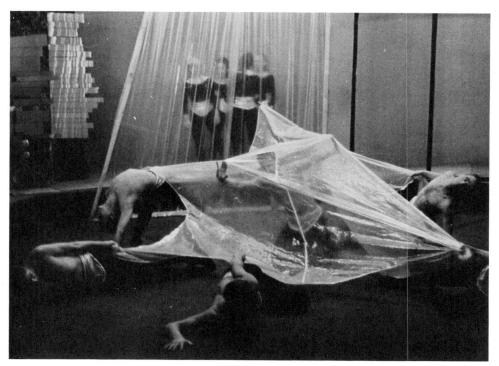

BALLET METAMORPHOSES. TV 1967. STAGE SETTINGS AND COSTUMES BY JÓZEF KALISZAN. CHOREOGRAPHY BY M. H. PRUSKA.

In the contest for the monument of "Fight and Martyrdom" in Bydgoszcz he achieved recognition. In October he became even more closely connected with Television-Poznan, assuming the post of permanent set designer for the Poznan region.

In 1965 an individual exhibition of sculpture hewn from copper was held in the ZPAP hall in Poznan.

He took part in an exhibition in Arezzo (Italy).

In 1966 the graphic cycle of "The Warsaw Ghetto" appeared. He took part in another exhibition in Arezzo (Italy).

He received the prize of the Committee for Radio and T.V. Affairs for his set design for the series of programs "Musical Sesame."

Ballet Metamorphoses. TV 1967. Stage Settings and Costumes by Józef Kaliszan. Choreography by M. H. Pruska.

TALES FROM THE "BOOK OF NIHONGA." TV BALLET IN 1966. STAGE SETTING
COSTUMES BY JÓZEF KALISZAN. CHOREOGRAPHY BY C. DRZEWIECKI.

SONG RECITAL BY W. DROJECKA, 1965. TV STAGE SETTING BY JÓZEF KALISZAN.

ASTROLABIUM. CONCRETE-GLASS, 1962.

In 1967 in March an individual exhibition of graphic arts was held in Poznan: Olgierd Blazewicz, a plastic arts critic of "The Voice of Greater Poland
(Glos Wielkopolski) wrote: "The newest works of Józef Kaliszan represent
dramatically different attitudes. Kaliszan, indeed, treats drawing not so
much in the category of sketches, impressions or jottings from live nature as
rather a comprehensive work, discerning and meaningful. He approaches
surrealism and expressionism, hence those movements in plastic arts which
afford the opportunity to reveal matters of content and expression. The
narrative drawings, which sometimes retain the story-telling sequence of
sections, have quite varied artistic value. The best from the plastic arts point
of view are unquestionably the plates — illustrations to the *Decameron*. The
most humanistic in their influence are the works from the pre-war series
1939-1945. Less convincing on the other hand are the color plates recap-

28

turing the style of German literary expressionism, resembling somewhat the posters which in works of this type is probably not creditable. In all, however, although quantitatively modest, the exhibition of drawings by Kaliszan deserves notice. One would like, however, to see a greater, more complete collection not only of the drawings but also the sculptures of this artist."

The series of illustrations to the *Decameron* was organized in honor of Boccacio at an exhibition in Florence (Italy).

In July he received recognition at a contest for a monument of Prince Przemyslaw I, founder of the city of Poznan.

LIST OF PAINTINGS

GHETTO FIGHTING

MASSACRE

EXODUS

Who Am I

1. After the Germans overran the country, the
Polish Jews were stunned, anticipating disaster; they already knew what had happened to
the Jews in Germany as a result of Hitler's
brutal anti-Semitism. If the answer to the question "Who Am I?" was, "A Jew," it meant
"condemned to annihilation." For according
to the words of Ley, one of the leading expo-
nents of Hitlerite ideology, "Europe can re-
gard the Jewish question settled only when the
last Jew leaves the continent . . . we swear that
we will not give up the struggle until the last
Jew in Europe perishes and we make sure that
he is dead indeed."

33

2. One of the first orders was to wear the Star of David on the breast, the back, or the sleeve (depending on the decision of the local German authorities). Oh, people of Israel, could you believe it? Synagogues desecrated; the Star of David becoming a stigma, a mark of identification, like the medieval bell of the leper; a sign of disgrace separating one from the rest of society, and in the end an advantage for one's persecutors.

34

Humiliation

3. An old tormented Jew, treated like a plaything by soldiers; Jewish scientists herded together to scrub streets; a rabbi with his hair crudely shaved; a circumcized boy placed naked in public; each of these humiliations was a typical act of German sadism.

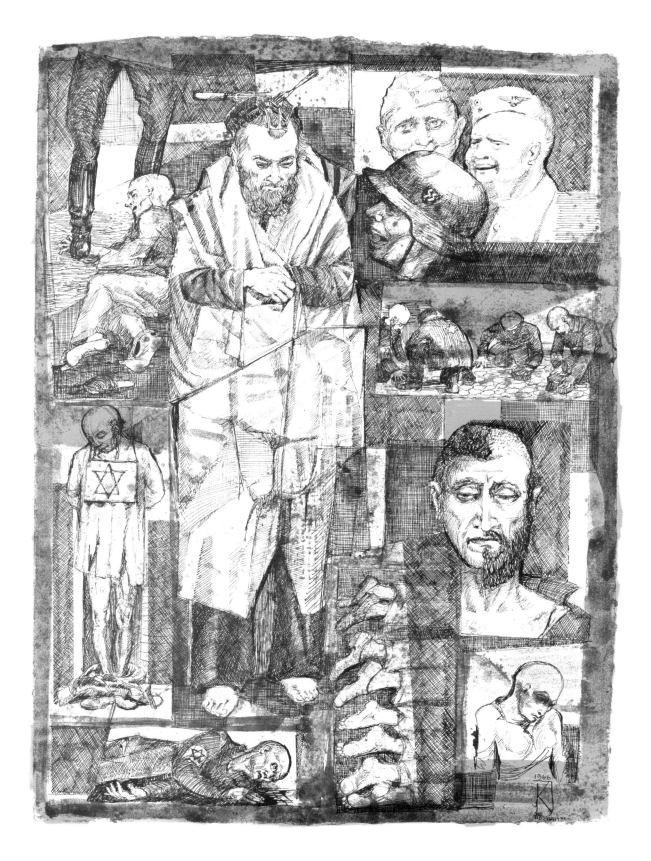

Cutting of the Hair

4. It was not in vain that Hitler boasted: "I freed the Germans from such stupid and degrading prejudices as conscience and morality . . . I want young people who are able to attack and to seize, to be relentless and cruel." An example of this upbringing was this painful head shaving, a complete abuse of human dignity. The Germans vied with each other in devising new ways of cutting the Jews' hair. Often, accompanied by roars of laughter, they would deprive the victim of just a certain portion of his hair. After the inside of his shop was demolished, the owner was shaved in this special way. Weights were added to the rest of his hair and he was thrown into the street to become an object of ridicule — a testimony to the complete immorality of his persecutors.

39

5. Germans schooled in anti-Semitism continued their monstrous task. Evil blew daily through German quarters, against the faces of the Jews. Robbery, destruction, assault, and brutality went unpunished amid the clatter of breaking windows and the cries of the victims.

ONE'S OWN LAND

6. All rights were taken away from the Jews. All
   they had left was the right to the soil — that
   very soil they dug with their bare hands for
   their own graves. Mass executions began.

EXODUS TO THE PROMISED LAND

7. The year was 1940. At first Jews evicted from
their homes believed the Germans when they
said that better conditions awaited them where
they were going. Once again in history they
were setting out on homeless wanderings; once
more loomed the hope of a promised land.

44

8. However, in spite of these reassurances, leaving a home ransacked by Germans spelled disaster. Carrying small bundles rescued before the pillage, uprooted from their daily lives, silent columns of Jews set out to meet what the fates had in store for them. But this time they were forced to accept an undeserved sentence.

46

47

Epitaph for Rachel of Kazimierz

9. Oh Rachel, young Jewess from the little shop in the Casimir Market, in those ghastly days your beauty grew sorrowful as if you suspected . . . . In memory of that night when German bayonets pierced your body, still unacquainted with love, each year, the hour before dawn, the little stone houses in the Casimir Market weep softly.

STRIPPED OF ILLUSIONS

10. The Germans plundered the houses, and even took personal belongings as the owners carried them out. Sealed up in trains, with hunger, thirst, and the sufferings of children, these were evils that could not be foreseen, for their cruelty transcended the bounds of human imagination. Now, stripped of their illusions, they realized that there was only one sentence for all: annihilation. In the words of Himmler: "All Jews we lay our hands on in this war will be exterminated without exception."

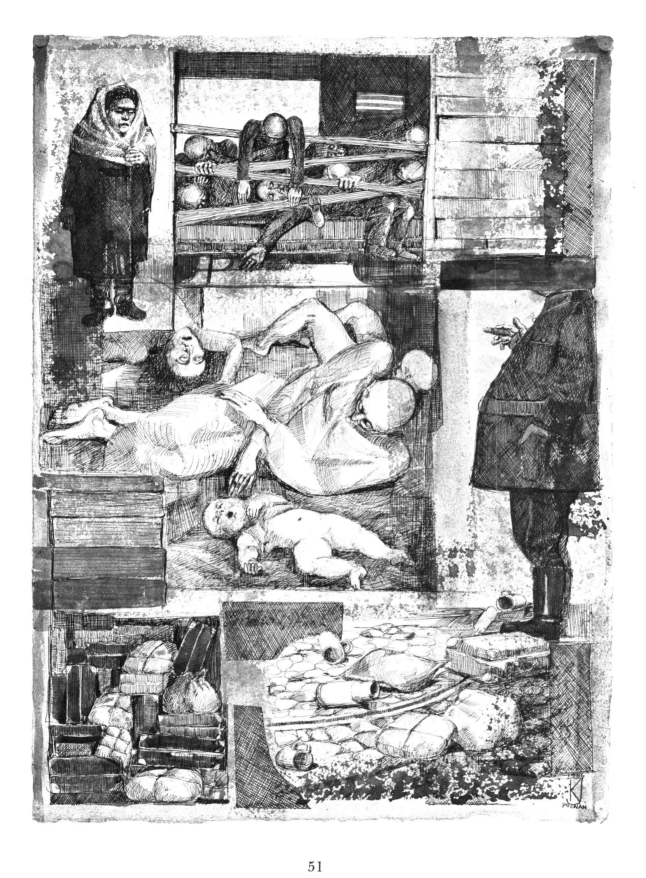

51

GHETTO

11. The Germans activated a plan to isolate the Jews completely from Aryan society. They herded them into one thickly populated sector and surrounded them with walls and barbed wire. The Aryan portion of a city terrorized by occupying forces, to those Jews locked up in the ghetto, seemed to be a world of free people, something precious lost forever.

I Will Follow My Way and You Take Yours

12. Passes issued at the beginning were withdrawn — the ghetto was locked to people from the outside and to those within. Mixed marriages suffered the tragedies of separation and an uncertain future. A single German command broke personal contacts and friendships. Defying the order which forbade crossing the border of the ghetto meant death. Those who were caught attempting to cross were hanged next to the walls as a warning to others (Warsaw), or their heads were impaled on the top of the walls (Lodz).

NEARER TO GOD

13. In the face of the suffering of those locked up in the ghetto, and in expectation of further persecutions, the tormented people of Israel felt nearer to God — and to death. Long prayers sustained their spirits, faith allowed them to bear the suffering and humiliation in peace. Before the inhuman abuse of the Germans the sound of the verses of the Talmud fortified them. All of those imprisoned needed faith that God did exist, in spite of all the evil that surrounded them.

THE INTERRUPTED PASSOVER

14. Goebbels described the ghettos thusly: "They are to be chambers of death." And so Hitler's henchmen carried out the harshest reprisals. On the days of the sabbath and the paschal they broke into the ghetto, assaulted the women, beat and killed the men, plundered and destroyed. For those imprisoned in the ghetto the nights were more dangerous than the days, and holidays worse than ordinary days. There was neither a safe place nor a safe moment on their side of the barrier.

58

The Poorest of the Poor

15. "When a child suffers, Heaven cries." And yet Heaven remained silent in the face of the sufferings of thousands of Jewish children against whom the decree of death was signed. The little faces of the older children were prematurely aged, and those of the younger ones were dull from hunger — this was a tragic sight in the everyday life of the ghetto.

    Every effort was made to hide their fate from the children. Janusz Korczak, a well-known teacher, was hiding it from his little group from the orphanage. All the children from his orphanage had been condemned to extinction in the gas chambers; for him, Aryan papers had been prepared, he was to remain free. He would not accept this gift. He remained with his charges to the end, telling stories in order to distract their attention from the taste and smell of gas. Since he could not save them from death, he accepted it with them.

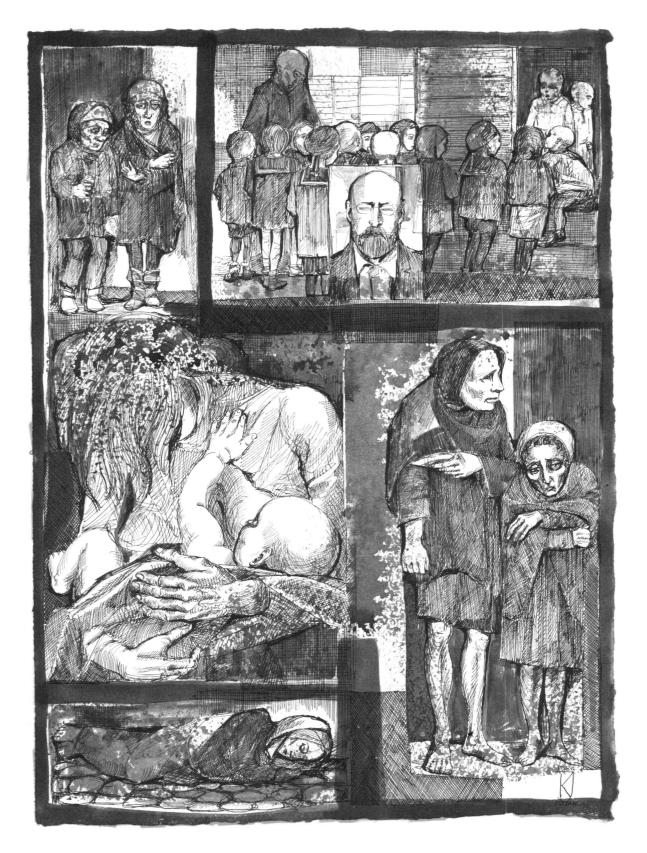

COAL MORE PRECIOUS THAN GOLD

16. The winter of the year 1942–43 was a further disaster for the inhabitants of the Warsaw ghetto. The lack of coal, not only for heating the living quarters, but above all for cooking, was an added burden. Furniture was chopped up and used as fuel, and even wooden stair rails were collected. It was impossible for the Jews to obtain coal, since it had achieved the value of the most precious jewel.

63

WORK MEANS LIFE

17. Every morning columns of men set out to work under German supervision. Those who hid in the houses were searched for and hunted down. The death penalty was declared for ignoring the duty of labor for the Germans. Hitler's program read: "He who has been condemned to extinction should before his death be not only completely destitute but should have been completely exploited."

65

PAVEMENTS

18. The cobblestones of the ghetto became the
final resting place for many Jews. Upon them
lay those who had been beaten during the numerous German "actions" or those exhausted
beyond human endurance from hard work or
starvation. Shots ringing out at night forecast
new corpses which were revealed by the dawn
rising over the streets of the ghetto.

66

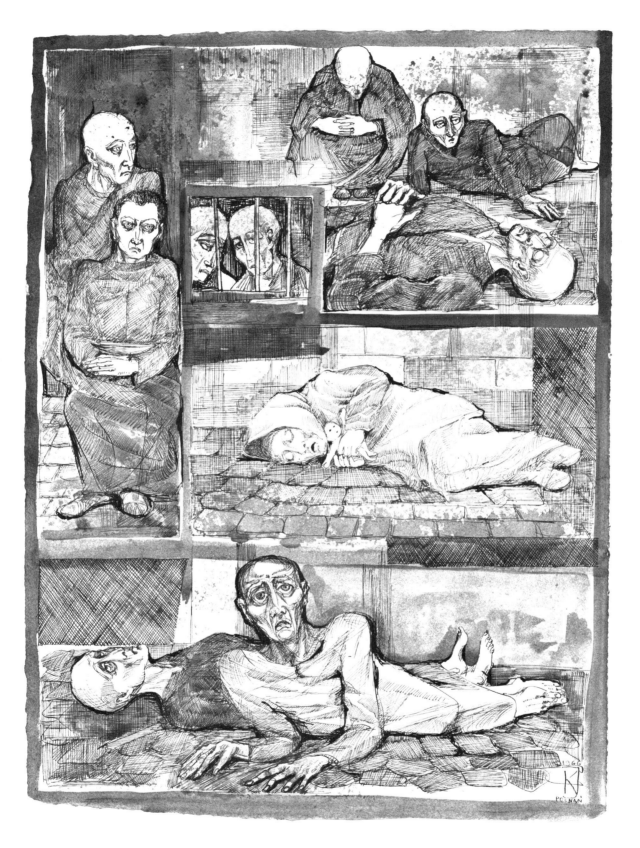

19. Transportation into the unknown continued. The only unknown factor was the actual place, since too quickly did the ghetto inhabitants realize that the concentration camp lay at the end of the journey, and there, indirectly, the gas chamber. Young, beautiful women were often selected from the trucks to be sent off to the brothels at the front, which prolonged their humiliation for a couple of weeks or months before the inevitable death. From the time of its establishment to its final collapse the Germans removed 300,000 persons to concentration camps from the Warsaw ghetto.

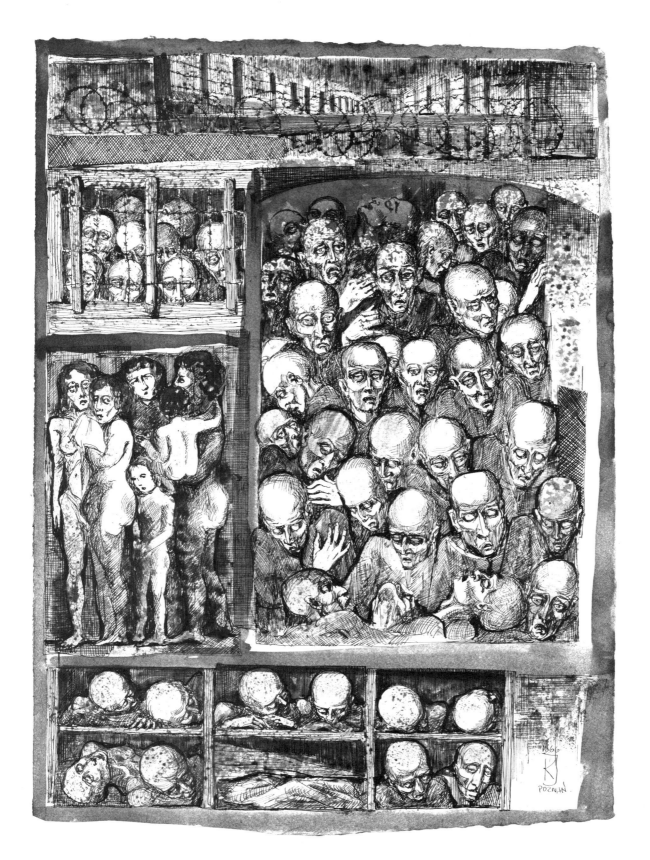

HUNGER

20. The Warsaw ghetto numbered about 500,000 persons toward the end. The population equalled 15 people per one liveable room. Under these conditions universal starvation reigned. The Germans were not interested in supplying food for the ghetto, and any attempt to slip out to the Aryan side for a morsel of food meant certain death. Starving children wandered like shadows near the walls, over which unknown passersby on the Aryan side tossed pieces of bread. But those guarding the walls shot indiscriminately, not only at those throwing the bundles but at those picking them up.

71

GHETTO FIGHTING

AND HE SAW HIS CLOSE FRIENDS DIE

21. On September 6, 1942, all inhabitants of the
ghetto remaining alive were herded by a couple
of units of Waffen S.S. into a block bounded
by four streets. Thus began the deportation —
a movement characterized by murder, looting
and beating. Families were separated; those
whom it did not please the "lords of creation"
to murder on the spot were divided into two
groups: the ones suitable for work were as-
signed to heavy, twelve-hour labor for German
firms inside the ghetto; the ones remaining de-
parted in cattle wagons to the death camps.
The 70,000 people remaining in the ghetto,
terrorized, decimated by starvation, were faced
continuously with the inhuman death of their
dear ones; it was a dreadful fate which fell to
the lot (as is already well known) of all Jews.

WE HAVE NOTHING TO LOSE

22. Those imprisoned in the ghetto frequently asked themselves, Do we have to die in this way? In November, 1942, the Jewish Fighting Organization came into being; the Jewish Military Union was also active. Arms were collected, and tunnels were dug to the Aryan side from where help was supposed to come in the form of arms from the Armia Krajowa (Home Army); but it was never enough for a lengthy resistance against the oppressors.

Meanwhile, Himmler issued an order to liquidate the Warsaw ghetto. Groups of Germans entering the territory of the ghetto for this purpose were greeted by gunfire and barricades. The Jewish rebels had decided not to surrender without a fight. The good organization of the defense, in spite of huge losses in men, resulted in the fact that after three days the Germans were compelled to interrupt the action and withdraw from the ghetto without completing even half of their order to remove the rest of the population to the death camps.

75

HEROISM OF DESPAIR

23. In April, 1943, General Stroop became the commander in charge of forcing the Jews out of the ghetto. The number and power of the adversary presupposed victory for the Germans — but what then? Those resisting in the ghetto realized that defeat would mean death not only for themselves but for the entire civilian population — women, children, sick, and old. In their fight against a fully armed enemy there was as much despair as heroism. The positions of those who fell or who were severely wounded in the battle were filled immediately by others for whom so far there had been no weapons. Frequently, without waiting for the actual death, a man would take the weapon of his dying brother and rush into the maelstrom of battle with eyes hardened by terror and determination.

WE DIE FIGHTING

24. And so the fight for the preservation of humanity rolled on — the fight for life; the fight for revenge for those who had already perished and for those who would. The fierce leader of the revolt was "Malachi" — Mordechaj Anielewicz. A few days of continuous fighting exhausted the insurgents; but it was also hard on the Germans who sustained great losses in men and tanks. Women also joined in the defense of the ghetto. Their courage and contempt for life stemmed from a deep hatred of the enemy, and this more than compensated for the weakness of their sex. Those of the rebels who perished at their posts died without compromising, without losing their pride or their dignity.

78

STREET BARRICADES

25. Although apparently terrorized for a long time, the ghetto showed that it too had fangs. Barricades arose as if from under the ground as a defense against the military logic of the Germans. It thus became impossible for the enemy to overcome the rebel resistance, until an order came from Himmler to set the ghetto on fire and blow up the buildings.

80

FLAMES, SMOKE

26. Flames leaped high above Warsaw. The ghetto
burned, set on fire by the Germans; German
stores in the area burned, set on fire by the
rebels. Airplanes bombed the ghetto with in-
cendiary bombs — more and more were killed
and wounded. In spite of the holocaust that
raged the resistance did not weaken. In the
period from the second week of the revolt to
May 8, the Germans were forced to fight scores
of battles, so great was the courage of the men
who remained alive.

MY HOUSE IS MY CASTLE

27. Since fires spread throughout almost the entire ghetto, every house became a sronghold. Inside the burned-out buildings cellars became the operational bases of the insurgents. The Germans combed each and every ruin as it was entered, since behind every corner might have lurked the gunfire of an insurgent.

Against the small groups of insurgents defending isolated positions the Germans threw artillery, airplanes, and tanks. Hard-fought battles took place around the bunker at 18 Mila Street, where the command of the Jewish Fighting Organization was situated. On May 8, 1943, the Germans captured the ruins of the bunker in which one hundred men of the insurrection staff, including its commander Mordechaj Anielewicz, perished.

85

DEATH ON THE PAVEMENT

28. The Germans ruthlessly carried out the order to annihilate the ghetto. Inside the burning houses the civilian population lived as in gehenna: many preferred to leap out of the windows of the burning houses to cut short their torments, rather than come out into the street against German gunfire. Even those who chose death by falling to the street were shot at as if they were still dangerous criminals. From Stroop's report: "It was possible to observe all the time that these Jewish criminals, in spite of their terror of the conflagration, preferred to turn back into the flames rather than fall into our hands . . ."

29. The participation of women in the insurrection was considerable. Consciously choosing the path of battle, by their example they boosted the morale of their comrades, bearing equally with them the terrible conditions of those days of the insurrection. Many of these young people perished. Death in battle is rather associated with men — so the heroes of the ghetto felt all the more bitter when young girls and women perished, flowers which in different conditions could still bloom and bring joy to their hearts. Their deaths, together with all the grief and suffering, increased the fighting spirit of the men and their desire for vengeance against the enemy.

The Last Prayer

30. In the cellars of the ruined houses the remnants of the civilian population offered up prayers to God — but He could not save them. They united with Him for the last time while awaiting destruction. The spiritual solemnity of these sad moments prepared the condemned · for their cruel fate.

Oh Jahwe, receive your children!

90

91

MASSACRE

SMALL CAPS

INCENDIARIES

31. Against a background of silent bunkers veiled
in fire and smoke, how cruel seemed the German arsonists who completed the act of destruction: those hated uniforms; those sadistic
faces; inhuman executors of inhuman orders;
units of S.S., S.D., Wehrmacht, Hitler's police
and auxiliary formations of S.S. comprising
Latvian and Ukrainian fascists.

93

ARTILLERY RANGE

32. The Nazis dragged the defenseless Jewish people out of the smoldering ruins and used them for humiliating diversions. By putting them against the wall, and using the Stars of David on their backs as targets, they improved the efficiency of their aim. But the condemned took their fate with human dignity.

So There Is No Mercy

33. The systematic emptying of the captured houses by the Germans always indicated new murders. Captured were those worn out by the purgatory they had undergone; often sick, wounded, or staggering, weak from starvation. Stroop's report of the action on April 25, 1943, rings cynically: "... altogether 1690 Jews were captured alive. Daily, many were blown up and buried in the bunkers, and, as far as is possible to ascertain, were burned. Not one of those captured was allowed to live."

CRIME WITHOUT PUNISHMENT

34. This unparalleled manslaughter of the defenseless Jewish population in the ghetto was
repeated daily, from the establishment of the
ghetto to its fall. In the middle of the twen-
tieth century, in civilized Europe, in the heart
of a capital city, crimes took place which elec-
trified the world, but a world which condoned
the criminals. In the course of the first five
days of the revolt nearly 20,000 men, women,
and children were shipped to the death camps.

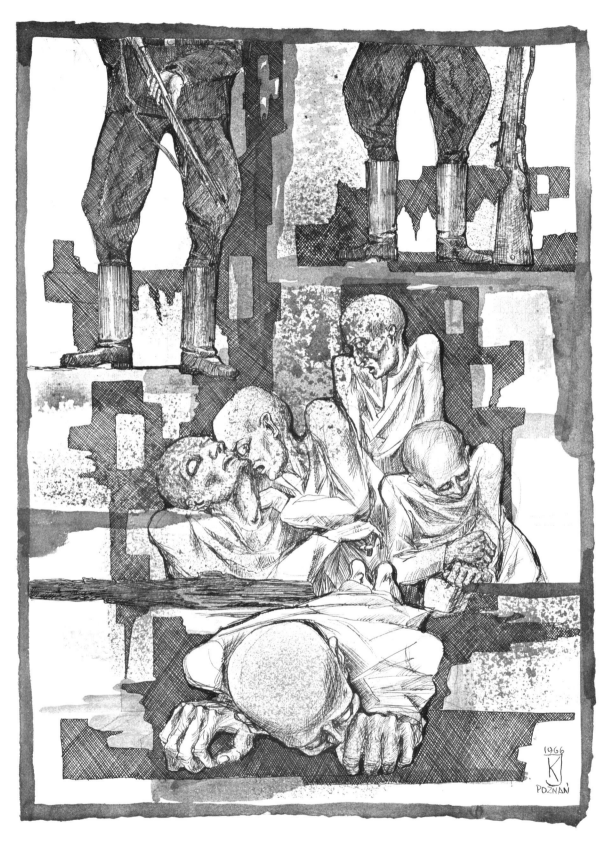

35. With the fierceness of bloodhounds the Germans infiltrated the ruins, dragging the people from concealment to be shot. They also surrounded the sewers, which were means of escape to the Aryan side. Some of the insurgents perished in those sewers when the Germans tossed bundles of grenades and injected gas through the holes. These experimental methods were employed later during the Warsaw uprising.

100

Leading Out

36. The inhabitants of the ghetto who were led out of the smoldering ruins had not seen daylight for a long time. Encountering the brightness of the day, however, signified not hope but the last chapter of their tormented life. The concept of humanitarianism became an abstraction for these poor souls, the same as the concept of "beauty" or "goodness." They emerged from hiding with dramatic evidence of a concentration against cruelty and evil, yet they were unable to resist these two forces.

103

37. Everyone captured by the Germans knew that he would perish. Old people, women, and children were condemned already. Sadistically, the Germans often made them stand for hours against a wall, waiting to be shot. This human tragedy did not move the henchmen carrying out the verdict in any way; it was a verdict against no other crime but their existence on earth.

104

105

A Death Transport

38. At first, shipments to the death camps were represented as deportations; but the last transportations out of the ghetto were made without pretence. Packed in sealed-up wagons, people were kept for many hours on sidings; the journey lasted many days. After opening the wagons the Germans looked with disgust at this act of destruction: the stench of dead bodies, the corpses which fell inertly, the people dying from long hours in the worst form of torture. Those remaining alive were herded with dogs and whips into the camps and gas chambers.

106

LIQUIDATED

39. Up to this day it is difficult to estimate the number of Jews murdered in the ghetto. More than 300,000 perished in the death camps; out of 70,000 living in the ghetto in September, 1942, after the insurrection and mass shootings, only a few thousand managed miraculously to save themselves. Of these, many perished during the Warsaw uprising and also in partisan fighting in various parts of the country.

What was cynically termed "liquidation" by the Nazis was and will be for the entire world a monstrous murder. This murder is recorded on the pages of history as a disgrace; the memory of those inhuman acts, the tortures and the murders, remains to prick the conscience of humanity.

109

It Is a Man Who Prepared Such a Lot for
Other Men

40. The territory of the ghetto in May, 1943,
showed a dead area, a field of smoldering ruins
with the skeletons of the burned-out houses
showing up dramatically. General of the S.S.
Jurgen Stroop reported with pride, "the Jewish sector has ceased to exist."

110

Es gibt keinen
jüdischen Wohnbezirk
– in Warschau mehr !

1966
POZNAN.

111